Echo-2

D1737079

Fast, Faster, Fastest

By Edward Radlauer

AN ELK GROVE BOOK

 CHILDRENS PRESS, CHICAGO

Library of Congress Cataloging in Publication Data

Radlauer, Edward.
  Fast, faster, fastest.

  (Ready, get set, go series)
  SUMMARY: Series of photographs of various kinds
of vehicles help demonstrate comparisons of their
speed, length, size, shape, and other characteristics.

  ''An Elk Grove book.''

  1. Racing—Juvenile literature. 2. Vehicles—Juvenile
literature. [1. Racing. 2. Vehicles]

I. Title.
GV1018.R32   796.7'2   73-6703
ISBN 0-516-07422-9

2 3 4 5 6 7 8 9 10 11 12 13 14 15 16 17 18 19 20 21 22 23 24 25 R 75 74 73

Ready, Get Set, Go Books

Ready
Motorcycle Mania

Get Set
Fast, Faster, Fastest

Go
Soap Box Racing

Fast, Faster, Fastest

A stock car is **fast.**

A funny car is fast, too.
A funny car is **faster** than a stock car.

A dragster is the **fastest.**
It's faster than a stock car or a funny car.
That makes a dragster the fastest.

Long, Longer, Longest

A dirt motorcycle is this **long.**

A chopper is **longer** than a dirt motorcycle.
What makes the chopper longer?

Is a drag racing motorcycle the **longest?**
It may not be the longest,
but it's the fastest.

Low, Lower, Lowest

Do you like this sport car? It's **low.**

A model car can be **lower** than a sport car.
You have to get down low to look at a lower car.

A low rider is lower than a sport car
or a model car. It's the **lowest.**
It has to be the lowest so it can be a low rider.

Short, Shorter, Shortest

How **short** can a bicycle be?

How short can a tricycle be?
Can it be **shorter** than a bicycle?

A unicycle must be the **shortest.**
It must be the shortest and slowest
because it's a unicycle.

High, Higher, Highest

Let's make a **high** motorcycle jump.

Let's make another jump.
Make it **higher** this time.

OK, that's the **highest** jump of all.
You can come down now.

Funny, Funnier, Funniest

A high old truck may look **funny.**

A VW van may look **funnier** than an old truck.
Is it funnier because it's higher or lower?

A custom car can look the **funniest.**
It may look the funniest
because it's higher and lower
all at the same time.

Strange, Stranger, Strangest

This car is **strange.** It wants to jump.

This **stranger** car doesn't want to jump.
It wants to bite a dog.

This is the **strangest** car.
It wants to bite a man.
Is that strange, stranger, or strangest?

Big, Bigger, Biggest

Minibike knobby tires are not very **big.**

These tires are **bigger** than minibike knobbies.
They are good for racing on dirt.

Which tire is the knobby?
Which tire is good for racing on dirt?
Which tire is the **biggest** of all?

Slow, Slower, Slowest

A boat with a broken engine gives a **slow** ride.

A wooden car gives a **slower** ride. If it isn't
a slower ride, the wooden car gets broken.

A motorcycle trials ride is the **slowest.**
If a trials ride isn't the slowest,
the motorcycle gets broken.

Square, Squarer, Squarest

Do you want a ride in an old **square** police car?

Or do you want a ride in an old dump truck?
It's **squarer** than a police car. It's slower, too.

Do you want a ride in a two-story bus?
Is it the **squarest?** Is a ride in the squarest
two-story bus better than a ride in a police car?

Round, Rounder, Roundest

A hot air balloon is sort of **round.** It's big, too.

Is a doughnut **rounder?** If you eat this doughnut, you'll feel bigger than a hot air balloon.

A racing slick has to be the **roundest.**
A slick has to be the roundest
so you can go the fastest.

Small, Smaller, Smallest

A midget car is **small.** It has a small engine.

Is a Soap Box car **smaller** than a midget car?
It needs a driver, but it doesn't have an engine.

Here's the **smallest** car. It's smaller
than a midget car or a Soap Box car.
Does the smallest car have a driver?

Old, Older, Oldest

Grandpa's motorcycle is **old,** and it's slow, too.

Grandpa's dragster is **older** than his motorcycle.
Is it slower, too?

Grandpa's car is the **oldest.**
Is it the oldest and the slowest?
Or is it the slowest and the oldest?

Wild, Wilder, Wildest

An old street roller is **wild.** It isn't very fast.

A custom woody is **wilder** than a street roller.
It's wilder and it's faster.

A bathtub car is the **wildest.** It's wilder
than a street roller or a custom woody.
Is the bathtub car fast, faster, fastest,
or is it wild, wilder, wildest?

Where to find . . .

Page

Big, Bigger, Biggest _____ 18

Fast, Faster, Fastest _____ 4

Funny, Funnier, Funniest _____ 14

High, Higher, Highest _____ 12

Long, Longer, Longest _____ 6

Low, Lower, Lowest _____ 8

Old, Older, Oldest _____ 28

Round, Rounder, Roundest _____ 24

Short, Shorter, Shortest _____ 10

Slow, Slower, Slowest _____ 20

Small, Smaller, Smallest _____ 26

Square, Squarer, Squarest _____ 22

Strange, Stranger, Strangest _____ 16

Wild, Wilder, Wildest _____ 30